PETER ELDIN

MATCH PLAY

Safe puzzles, games and tricks with matchsticks

Illustrated by
Pinpoint Design Company

A DRAGON BOOK

GRANADA

London Toronto Sydney New York

Published by Granada Publishing Limited in 1982

ISBN 0 583 305 10 5

Copyright ©Eldin Editorial Services 1982

Granada Publishing Limited
Frogmore, St Albans, Herts AL2 2NF
and
36 Golden Square, London W1R 4AH
866 United Nations Plaza, New York, NY 10017, USA
117 York Street, Sydney, NSW 2000, Australia
100 Skyway Avenue, Rexdale, Ontario M9W 3A6, Canada
61 Beach Road, Auckland, New Zealand

Printed and bound in Great Britain
by Cox & Wyman Ltd, Reading

Granada ®
Granada Publishing ®

Contents

INTRODUCTION	5
SQUARES AND TRIANGLES	7
ROMAN ARITHMETIC	21
PERPLEXING PROBLEMS	27
NIFTY STUNTS	43
MAGIC WITH MATCHES	53
MATCH PLAY	81
THE ANSWERS	95

Introduction

When I was about twelve years of age, I read about an old-time magician called Jack Le Dair who performed match puzzles on the music hall stage. It seemed such a good idea that I immediately went out and bought some balsa wood to make giant matches so that I could put on my own match puzzle act. At the time I thought that my act would take the world by storm but for some, now forgotten, reason, that act never did materialize. No doubt I discovered some other equally important pastime over which to enthuse.

Although my match puzzle act never came to anything, reading about Jack Le Dair did spark off an interest in tricks and puzzles with matches that has lasted to the present day. Over the years I have built up quite a collection of things to do with matches which I hoped one day I would publish as a book. That day has now arrived and I am pleased to offer you a selection of items from my collection which I hope you will find interesting, intriguing, and amusing.

In compiling this collection I have left out puzzles that require more than a basic knowledge of mathematics and tricks that require an expert knowledge of magic. Neither will you find any magic tricks that use finger wrenching sleight of hand.

I have also left out of this book those tricks which require the matches to be ignited. *Matches are dangerous*. Although this book is concerned with matches I would recommend that you use a substitute wherever possible. Most of the tricks and puzzles in this book work equally well with drinking straws, toothpicks, pieces of chalk, or crayons. If you do use matches you must use dead ones as there is then no risk whatsoever of something or someone getting burned. Ask your friends and relatives to save their dead matches for you, it will not be long before you collect enough to do everything described in this book.

I got a lot of pleasure from writing this book, I hope you get a great deal of pleasure from trying out the various things I have described.

Peter Eldin

SQUARES AND TRIANGLES

FIVE FROM FOUR

Position sixteen matches to form five squares as shown. Can you move three matches so that the figure is now composed of four squares?

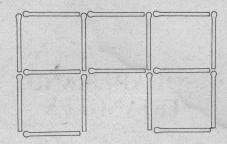

REMOVE FOUR TO MAKE FOUR

Arrange sixteen matches to form the figure shown in the illustration. Can you now take away four matches and leave four triangles?

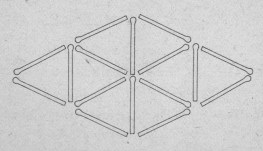

FOUR FROM FIVE

Form five squares with sixteen matches as shown. Now see if you can, by moving two matches only, form four squares.

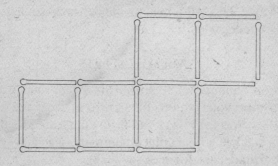

ALL SQUARE

Arrange twelve matches to form five squares as shown. Yes, there are five squares — four small ones and a fifth, larger one, formed by the eight outer matches.

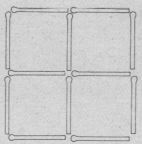

Using this figure as a base each time see if you can solve the following problems:

a   Remove two matches and leave two squares.
b   Move two matches and make six squares.

c Move two matches to make seven squares.
d Move three matches to make three squares.
e Move four matches to make two squares.
f Move four matches to make three squares.
g Move four matches to make ten squares.
h Move two matches to make three squares and six rectangles.

MATCH MAZE

Position 35 matches to form this maze. I will not ask you to find your way to the centre of the maze — that would be too easy! Try the following instead — move four matches and replace them in such a way that three squares are formed.

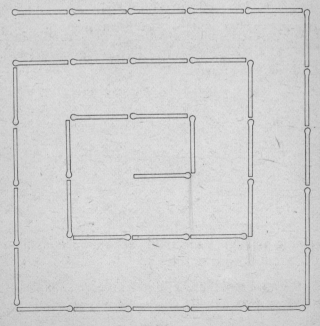

FIVE TO THREE

Arrange fifteen matches to form six squares as shown. Can you now remove three matches in such a way that you leave three squares?

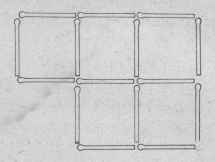

SIX FROM A GRID

These six puzzles all start with the same arrangement of matches. Position twenty four matches so they form a grid as shown below.

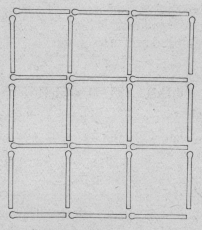

Can you now do any of the following?

a   Take away four matches and leave five squares.
b   Take away six matches and leave three squares.
c   Take away six matches and leave five squares.
d   Take away eight matches and leave two squares.
e   Take away eight matches and leave three squares.
f   Take away eight matches and leave four squares.

JUST TWENTY FOUR

Take twenty four matches and see if you can arrange them to form the following:

a   Four squares.
b   Five squares.
c   Six squares.
d   Seven squares.
e   Nine squares.
f   Ten squares.
g   Fourteen squares.
h   Forty two squares.
i   One hundred and ten squares!

ELIMINATE THE SQUARES

Place forty matches on a table to form the figure shown opposite. There are now two problems to solve.

a   How many squares are there?
b   What is the least number of matches you have to remove to leave no squares whatsoever?

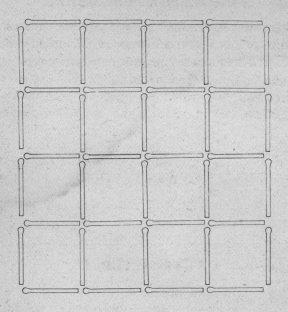

THREE TO TWO

Arrange seven matches to form three triangles as shown. Can you now reduce the number of triangles from three to two by moving just two matches?

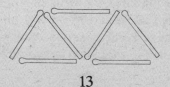

TRIANGLES IN A HEXAGON

Arrange twelve matches to form six equilateral triangles in a hexagon as shown. Can you now move four matches to make three equilateral triangles?

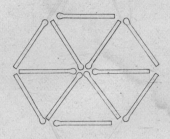

FIVE FROM THREE

Put down nine matches to form three triangles as shown. By moving just three matches can you make five triangles?

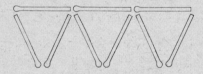

SOLOMON'S SEAL

Use eighteen matches to form the figure known as Solomon's Seal as shown. You will observe that the design consists of eight triangles. Can you now move just two matches so that six triangles are left?

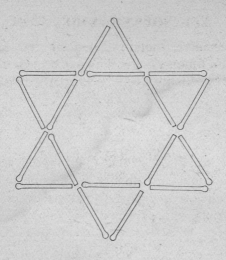

A TRICKY PROBLEM

Can you arrange six matches in such a way that three squares of equal size are formed?

Be careful for, as the title implies, there is a trick to this one.

REMOVE THREE TO MAKE THREE

Arrange thirteen matches to form the shape shown in the illustration. Now see if you can take away three matches to leave three triangles.

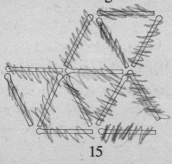

15

SQUARE TRICK

Can you arrange fifteen matches on a table so as to form eleven squares?

AXE TRIANGLES

Make the outline of an axe using nine matches as shown. Can you now move five matches in such a way that five triangles are formed?

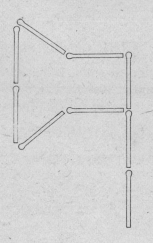

DIAMOND DAZZLER

How can you arrange twelve matches so that seven diamonds are formed? You are not allowed to break any of the matches.

TURN THE L

Arrange ten matches to form the L shape shown in the illustration. Can you now turn the L upside down by moving only two matches?

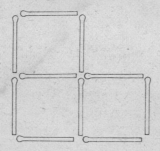

HOW TO MAKE DIAMONDS

Place twelve matches on a table so that they form the shape, composed of six triangles, in the illustration. Can you now move four matches in such a way that five diamond shapes are formed?

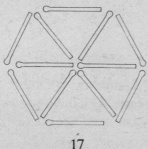

MAKE NINE

Arrange thirty-six matches to form the pattern of squares shown below. The problem now is to take away only four matches and yet leave nine squares.

TRICKY TRIANGLE

Can you form a triangle using only one match? You are not allowed to bend or break the match.

TRICKY SQUARE

If you solved the last problem (or if you have already looked up the answer) you will find this tricky square very easy for it is based on the same principle. This time you have to form a square using just two matches. Again, you are not allowed to bend or break the matches.

SQUARES AND TRIANGLES

Can you place eight matches down on a table in such a manner that the figure so formed contains two squares and four triangles?

ROMAN ARITHMETIC

ROMAN ARITHMETIC

As you are no doubt aware, it is possible to represent Roman numbers with matches as illustrated below.

The problems in this section all make use of this fact but in order to keep things relatively simple, mainly for the author's benefit, only the numbers from one to twelve have been used.

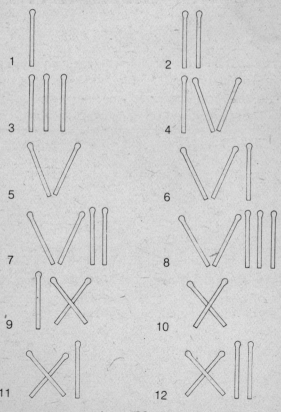

4−2=5

With ten matches form the equation, in Roman numerals, 4 − 2 = 5. This is, of course wrong. Can you put it right by moving just one match?

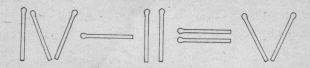

3=1

Place six matches on the table to form the equation 3 = 1 in Roman numerals. Now see if by moving two of the matches, you can make the equation read correctly. There are several possible answers to this one.

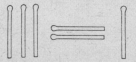

3 − 2 = 4

Arrange eleven matches to form the equation in Roman numerals, 3 − 2 = 4. By moving one match you can make the equation read correctly?

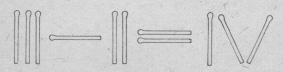

6 − 4 = 9

With twelve matches form the equation 6 − 4 = **9** in Roman numerals. By moving just one match can you make the equation read correctly? There are two possible solutions.

1 − 3 = 2

Arrange nine matches to form the equation 1 − 3 = 2. Can you now move one match to make the equation correct?

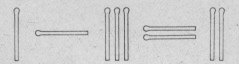

7 − 2 = 2

Place eleven matches to form the equation 7 − 2 = 2. By moving just two matches can you make the equation a valid one?

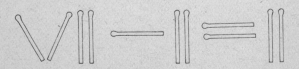

11 + 1 = 10

Place ten matches on a table to form the equation 11 + 1 = 10. Once again your problem is how to make the equation valid. But this time you are not allowed to touch any of the matches.

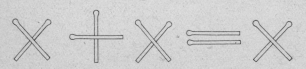

7 − 1 = 1

Arrange nine matches to form the equation, in Roman numerals, 7 − 1 = 1. By taking away just two matches can you form an equation that is correct?

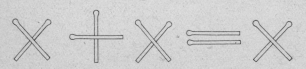

10 + 10 = 10

Here is yet another problem that requires you to make both sides of the equation equal. This time you must move two matches.

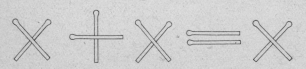

$$6 + 2 = 5$$

Can you make both sides of this equation equal by moving just one match? See if you can find two solutions to the problem.

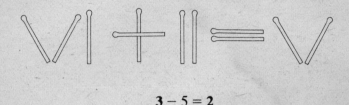

$$3 - 5 = 2$$

Arrange ten matches to form the equation $3 - 5 = 2$. By moving only one match can you make the equation balance?

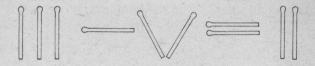

HALF A DOZEN

With matches it is possible to prove that half of twelve is seven. How?

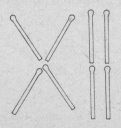

PERPLEXING
PROBLEMS

THE BUILDING PLOT

A builder has bought the building plot represented with matches in the illustration. He wishes to divide the site into three plots each the same size and shape. With just eight additional matches can you show how this could be done?

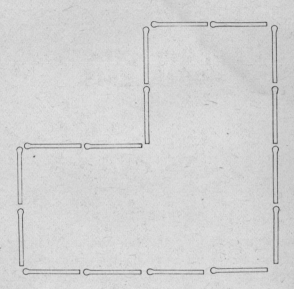

TREASURE ISLAND

The matches in the illustration represent a lake with an island in its centre. There is treasure on the island and you wish to get to it. You have only two matches with which to build a practical bridge. How do you do it?

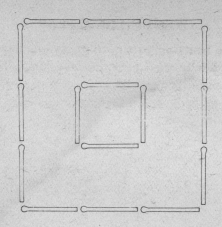

ANOTHER BRIDGE

Place four matches more than the length of a match apart on a table to represent the banks of a river as shown. With just four additional matches can you form a practical bridge that crosses from one bank to the other?

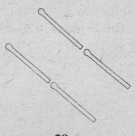

WITHIN THE TREES

Place eight matches and four coins on the table as shown. The matches represent a lake in a park and the coins represent trees.

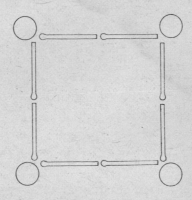

One day the park keeper decided it would be nice to double the size of the lake. His supervisors agreed that it would be pleasant to have a larger lake but insisted that it had to remain square in shape and that it had to be contained within the confines of the four trees. It was further stipulated that the trees were not to be moved.

The park keeper scratched his head for a while but eventually solved the problem. He made a square lake twice the size of the original, and the trees remained where they were on the edges of the lake. How did he do it?

REMOVE THE STRAW

Place four matches on the table to form the shape of a wine glass. A fifth match is placed into the glass to represent a straw.

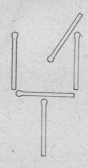

The problem is to get the straw out of the glass without moving it. You are, however, permitted to move just two of the matches that form the glass but after these two moves the glass must remain intact.

CROSS SOLITAIRE

Lay down eight matches in a row. Now pick up a match, pass it over two other matches, and lay it across the next match. Can you now continue in the same manner until you have four crosses? One small point — you are allowed to move only four matches to do this.

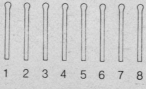

1 2 3 4 5 6 7 8

TREE TROUBLE

Arrange twenty two matches to form a rectangle. Place four coins in the positions shown. The figure represents an area of land upon which there are four trees, represented by the coins. This land belonged to a man who bequeathed it to his four sons. The man

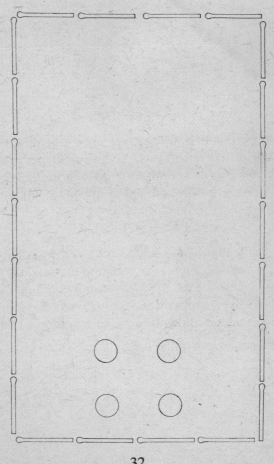

said that the four boys were to divide the land equally between them so that they each had a plot of land of exactly the same shape and size. He further stipulated that each plot had to contain one of the trees and that the trees were not to be moved.

How was the land divided?

FOUR PILES

Place twelve matches in a row on the table. By moving eight of the matches one at a time can you form them into four groups each of three matches? Each time you move a match it must pass over three matches before it is replaced on the table.

FOUR PAIRS

Place eight matches in a row upon the table. Can you now move the matches so they form four pairs? In doing this you must obey the rule that each match that is moved must be passed over two other matches before it is replaced on the table.

EVEN REMOVAL

Place thirty-six matches on a table in six rows each of six matches. Can you now take away six of the matches in such a way that the rows that remain all contain an even number of matches whether counted horizontally, vertically, or diagonally?

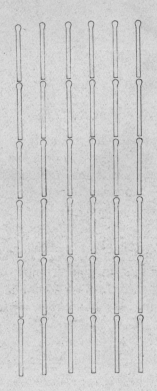

HELP!

Arrange fifteen matches to form the number 999. This number is used in the British Isles for emergency telephone calls. Usually such calls are an appeal for help. By adding one match and moving three matches can you change the number 999 into another appeal for help?

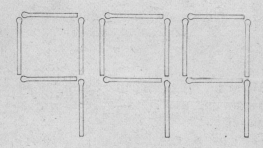

OIL TO INK

When you try this on your friends do not mention matches in any way. Just ask someone if it is possible to turn oil into ink. Whatever their reply you state that you can do so. You then arrange seven matches to form the word oil. Now simply rearrange the matches into the word ink. You have thus changed oil into ink.

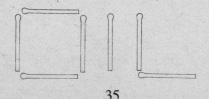

MATCHEMATICS

Place eight matches down to form the number 140 as shown. Now see if you can solve the following problems all of which start from this number. You are not allowed to make use of Roman numerals in solving any of these problems.

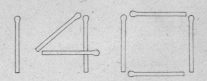

a   Move one match to make a sum that equals four.
b   Move one match to make a sum that equals eleven.
c   Move two matches to make a sum that equals one.
d   Move two matches to make a sum that equals ten.
e   Move two matches to make a sum that equals 25.
f   Move two matches to make a sum that equals 103.
g   Move two matches to make a sum that equals 111.
h   Move two matches to make a sum that equals 154.
i   Move two matches to make a sum that equals 412.

ARITHMATCHIC

With six matches form the sum 14 − 1 which, of course, equals 13. Can you move just one match to form a sum, the answer to which is 5?

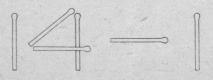

36

5 + 4 = 6

Arrange seventeen matches to form the equation 5 + 4 = 6. Now see if you can do the two problems that follow.

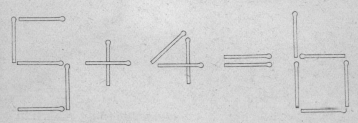

a   Move one match to make the equation read correctly.

b   Move two matches to form a correct equation.

2 + 9 = 8

With twenty one matches form the equation 2 + 9 = 8 as shown. Can you now make the equation read correctly by moving just one match?

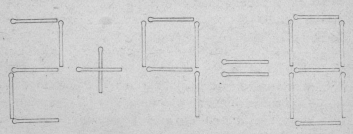

3 + 2 = 6

With nineteen matches form the equation 3 + 2 = 6. Can you make the equation read correctly by moving just one match?

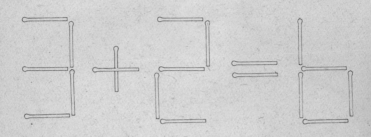

6 + 3 = 3

Place nineteen matches down on a table to form the equation 6 + 3 = 3. Now see if you can make correct equations keeping to the following instructions.

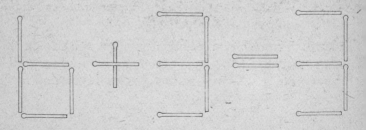

a   Move one match to make a correct equation.
b   Take away one match to make a correct equation.
c   Move four matches to make a correct equation.

2 + 1 = 8

Arrange seventeen matches to form the equation 2 + 1 = 8.

Can you now take away two matches to make the equation read correctly?

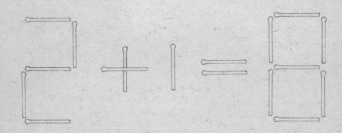

DO NOT TOUCH

Can you lay three matches on the table in such a manner that the heads do not touch the table top?

When you have done that, or when you have given up, see if you can do the same with four matches and then with six matches.

PENS FOR PIGS

Farmer Brown had six pigs which were each housed in a separate sty. The pieces of fencing he used to build the stys are represented by matches in the illustration.

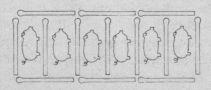

39

One day one of the pigs knocked into a piece of fencing and broke it. Farmer Brown was now faced with the problem of how to keep his six pigs in six pens using only twelve lengths of fencing instead of thirteen. Eventually he solved the problem, but can you?

Remove one of the matches and see if you can rearrange the remaining twelve matches to form six enclosures.

UPS AND DOWNS

Place eight matches in a row on the table. The heads of four matches point upwards and the other four point downwards. They are arranged alternately up and down as shown.

Now, by moving two adjacent matches at a time can you bring the up matches and the down matches together? You are allowed only four moves.

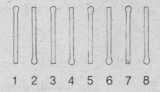

1 2 3 4 5 6 7 8

COIN MATCH

Can you place four matches on a table and place a coin on the matches in such a way that the coin touches each of the matches? That sounds easy — but there is a further stipulation. Neither the coin nor the match heads are allowed to touch the table.

40

A NEAT TOUCH

Can you arrange six matches in such a way that each match touches all of the other five matches?

GROUPS OF THREE

Place fifteen matches in a row. Can you now rearrange the matches into five groups of three matches each by picking up one match, passing it over three matches, and then placing it down, continuing in this fashion until the five groups are formed?

A FARMER'S PROBLEM

This is a farm. The small square is the farmhouse. The farmer wishes to divide the farm into five plots. Each plot has to be the same size and shape. Using additional matches can you establish how the land should be divided?

ANOTHER PROBLEM FOR ANOTHER FARMER

This is the farm next door to the farm in the last problem. When he saw that his friend had divided his land into five fields the second farmer decided to go one better and divide his land into six fields, each of the same shape and size. How did he do it?

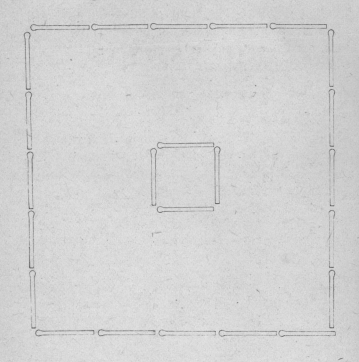

MORE FIELDS

With a little more thought the farmer in the last problem could have divided his land into eight fields all the same shape and size. How?

NIFTY STUNTS

STAR TURN

Bend six matches in the centre. Do not actually break them completely in half. Now place them down so they form a Maltese Cross as shown.

Without touching any of the matches can you now rearrange them so that they form a star?

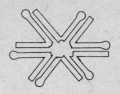

ROBBING THE BANK

Arrange four matches in a square to represent a bank and place a small coin in its centre as shown. Can you now get the money out of the bank without touching the coin or the matches?

ICE PICK

Place an ice cube into a glass of water. Now challenge anyone to lift the ice from the water with a matchstick.

Try as they may everyone will find that such a task is absolutely impossible.

But — with a little know how — you can do it!

A TRICKY ONE

Place eleven matches on the table. Take away five matches. Can you now add four matches and yet have nine left?

TRIANGLE TEASER

Place three matches on the table to form a triangle. Now position three additional matches in such a way that a total of four triangles are formed. Each of the additional matches must touch at least one of the matches already placed on the table.

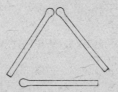

ABSOLUTELY NOTHING

Place six matches on a table in a row as shown. Now move two matches and leave nothing.

IMPOSSIBLE SQUARE

Arrange four matches to form a cross as shown. You now have to make a square. The only problem is that you are allowed to move only one match.

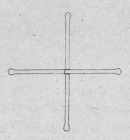

IMPOSSIBLE LIFT

Can you place eight matches on a table in such a way that you can lift them all at once with a ninth match?

MATCH YOUR STRENGTH

Ask someone to place a match in their fingers as shown in the illustration. Now challenge them to break the match with their fingers.

Not many people can do it and those who do succeed will find it quite difficult.

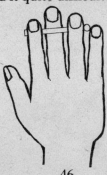

NUMBER PROBLEMS

Here are four puzzles each of which uses the same technique to achieve the answer. Once you realise what that technique is you should have no difficulty in solving all of them. If you try them out on your friends do not present them together as I have done.

Place 12 matches in a row on a table. Now see if you can do the following.

a   Take one match from the twelve and make one.
b   Take one match from the twelve and make nine.
c   Take two matches from the twelve and make five.
d   Take three matches from the twelve and make ten.

LIFT THEM

Get an adult to make a short split in the non-striking end of a match. Now wedge another match into the split at an angle to form the shape of a letter V. Place the V upside down on a table and lean a third match against them so they stand up as shown.

Can you not lift the three matches from the table using just one more match?

CRAFTY LIFT

How can you lift a pile of matches with just one additional match?

OPEN UP

Break a match almost in half (do not break it completely) and place it on the top of a bottle. Place a coin on top of the match (the coin must be smaller than the open top of the bottle). Now challenge a friend to cause the coin to drop into the bottle. No-one is allowed to touch the coin, the match, or the bottle.

But before challenging a friend see if you can solve the problem.

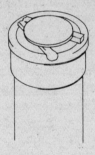

PULSE STICK

Push a drawing pin into one end of a matchstick. Using the drawing pin as a base balance the match on the underside of your wrist as shown. The match will now begin to move in time with the beat of your pulse.

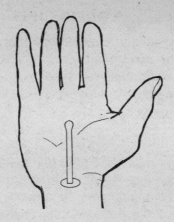

UPRIGHT FLOATER

Can you place a match into a tumbler of water in such a way that it will float in a vertical position?

If you put this question to your friends they may try to do it but will eventually have to admit defeat. This is not very surprising for it is impossible — unless you cheat! All you have to do is to push a pin into the end of the match. Place the match in the water and the weight of the pin will cause it to float in an upright position.

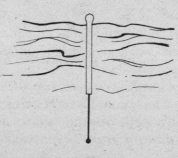

MATCH BRIDGE

Place three cups or glasses together as shown. With just three matches see if you can construct a practical bridge to connect each of the cups. The bridge should be solid enough to support a few coins or a small weight. Help is on page 128!

AMAZING MATCH BRIDGE

To build this match bridge requires quite a bit of patience. You will find the longer the matches you use the easier is the construction of the bridge. Even so, it still requires a steady hand.

The matches have to be put together in the order shown in the illustration. Place match 1 on the table. On this, and at right angles to it, place matches 2 and 3. Lay match 4 across the last two matches.

So far so good, but now things start getting a little tricky. With the thumb and forefinger of one hand lift match 1. Slide matches 5 and 6 under 1 and over 4. Now place match 7 on top of and match 8 underneath 5 and 6. Lift match 8 as you did earlier with match 1 and slide in matches 9 and 10 as shown. Continue in this manner until you run out of matches, or patience, or both.

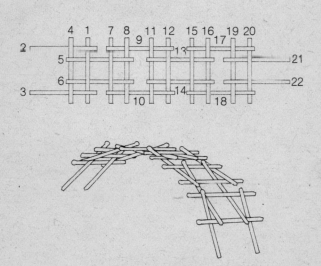

TRICKY TURNOVER

Clench your fists together and hold them side by side. Ask someone to push a match head first into your right fist and a second match with the head uppermost into your left fist. It is obvious to everyone watching that the heads are pointing in opposite directions.

Now knock your fists together a couple of times and then move them around each other in a circular motion. Tap both fists on the table and then open the hands, palm uppermost, side by side. Remarkable as it may sound, both matches now point in the same direction!

The secret? There is no secret, it works by itself. The whole thing is simple and yet it can fool some very clever people.

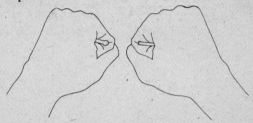

MAGIC WITH
MATCHES

INCREDIBLE BALANCE

When you bet your friends they cannot stand a match upright on a matchbox they will try and fail. But you can do it quite easily with a little secret assistance. This comes from a drawing pin which is pushed through the sleeve of the matchbox from the inside. To make the match stand upright on the box you secretly impale it upon the protruding part of the pin.

TRICKY TRANSPOSITION

Remove four matches from a box. Ask a spectator to place one match on your left palm and one on your right palm. Close your hands. Now ask the spectator to put one match across your left fingernails and the last match across your right fingernails.

You now turn your hands over and the two matches that were resting on your nails fall off on to the table. That, at least, is what the audience believes to have happened. What you really do as you turn your hands over is to open the right hand slightly so both the match on the nails and the match in the hand fall to the table. At the same time the left hand opens slightly to catch the match resting on the left nails. There are now two matches in the left hand and none in the right but the spectators believe there is still just one match in each hand.

Keeping the fists closed turn both hands over so the fingernails are uppermost once again. Ask the spectator to replace the dropped matches on the fingernails, one on each hand as before. You now explain that you are going to turn the hands over again but this time you will catch the loose matches — and that is exactly what you do.

The audience think there are two matches in each hand but when you open your hands there is one match in the right hand and three in the left!

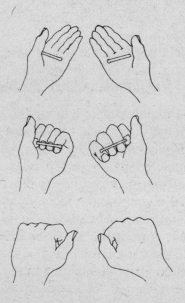

UNBREAKABLE MATCH

In this trick you place a match within the folds of a handkerchief and then invite someone to break the match through the material. It is obvious to everyone that the match is well and truly broken, but you then shake it from the handkerchief and it is seen to be whole once again − restored by your remarkable magical powers.

The secret lies in the fact that you have a second match hidden in the hem of the handkerchief and it is this match that gets broken.

Show the first match and openly place it beneath the handkerchief. In the same movement take the corner that has the match hidden in the hem up into the centre of the handkerchief. Allow someone to feel this match through the material and then to break it.

All you now have to do is make some suitable magical incantations and shake the first match from the hankerchief. It looks as if you have restored the match by magic and as the broken match remains hidden in the hem no-one will be any the wiser.

match concealed in hem of handkerchief

ANOTHER UNBREAKABLE MATCH

It must be admitted that the last trick is fairly well known. It is, therefore, useful to learn the following method for those occasions when you may have some knowing ones in your audience.

The effect is the same as before but the handkerchief is completely unprepared. It may even be done with a borrowed handkerchief if you wish.

Once again you make use of a duplicate match but this time it is hidden in the end of your tie (or scarf). As you take the visible match beneath the handkerchief you take the end of your tie also and the working for the rest of the trick is exactly as before.

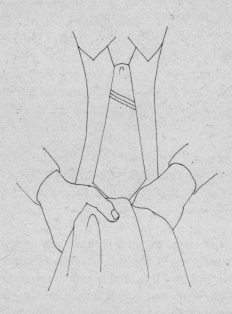

THE APPEARING MATCHES

Before showing this trick to anyone you must first prepare a matchbox by cutting the drawer in half. Replace both halves of the drawer in the sleeve and fill it with matches.

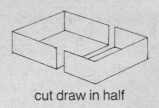

cut draw in half

To show the trick you pull up the top of the drawer. As the drawer is in two halves the matches remain hidden within the sleeve and the box appears to be empty.

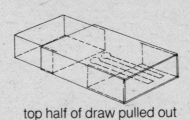

top half of draw pulled out

Close the drawer and make some appropriate magical passes over the box. You now open the box once again but this time you push the drawer up from the bottom. This time both halves of the drawer are pushed up and the once empty box is now filled with matches.

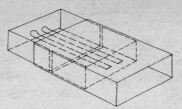

push drawer from bottom
and matches appear

PULL APART

For this trick you will need just two matches and a little practice. Place one match in the thumb crotch of each hand with the heads towards the palm of the hand as shown.

Bring the two hands together. Twist them slightly so you can grasp each match between the thumb and forefinger of the opposite hand. The thumbs should be against the head of each match.

At first you may find it awkward to attain this position naturally, but after a little practice you should find it a lot easier.

Now grip the matches firmly and with a twisting movement draw the hands apart.

The spectators receive the impression that the matches have passed through each other. When they try for themselves they find that it just cannot be done.

Even when you repeat the trick, and the movements appear to be absolutely fair, no one will be able to duplicate your actions.

ANTI-MAGNETIC MATCHES

For this trick you will need two matches. Place one on the palm of your left hand so that about half of its length projects away from the hand. The right hand now brings the second match up close to the first. But as the matches are about to make contact the one on the left hand suddenly flies up in the air as if propelled by some magnetic force.

What actually happens is that the right hand flicks its match at the appropriate moment and it is the sudden contact with the left hand match that causes it to leap into the air. To do this hold the match between the right finger and thumb near the head end as shown in the illustration. Bring this match up to the first. As they are about to touch click the nail of the right third finger against the end of its match. This secret movement is not seen by the audience neither is the resultant movement of the head end of the match but the sharp impact is sufficient to knock the left hand match way up into the air.

It may sound rather a simple stunt but some of the simplest things in magic are also the most effective. This one certainly is. Just try it and see.

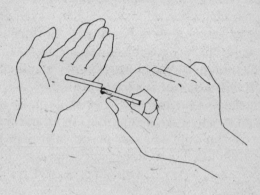

THE VANISHING MATCH

You place a match on the palm of your hand and then cover it with a handkerchief. Several spectators are then allowed to reach under the handkerchief one by one to make sure the match is still there. But when you whip the handkerchief away the match has completely disappeared!

No, it is not up your sleeve. In fact you could do this trick wearing just a bathing costume if you wished. The secret of the trick is that the last person to feel beneath the handkerchief is your secret assistant. He or she simply removes the match from your palm unbeknown to the rest of the audience!

CATCH THE MATCH

A match and three cups are placed down on the table. You now turn your back and invite someone to place the match beneath one of the cups. When you turn back you can reveal immediately which cup conceals the match. When you have repeated this performance a few times everyone will be convinced that you possess uncanny psychic powers.

The secret is ridiculously simple. But do not dismiss it on that account for some of the simplest tricks are also the best. One of the spectators is your secret assistant who uses a simple code to indicate which is the chosen cup. He just points at it with his feet as shown in the illustration!

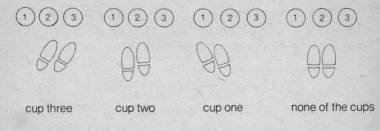

cup three   cup two   cup one   none of the cups

There may be occasions when a spectator will try to catch you by not putting the match under any of the cups. All your assistant has to do on this occasion is stand with his feet together and you will know what has taken place.

WAND CONTROL

About six matches are placed on the surface of some water. When the magician touches the water with his wand the matches move away towards the edge of the bowl. The magician touches the water with the wand once again and as if controlled by some unseen force, the matches float back towards the centre.

As you may have gathered, the secret lies in the wand. It is, in reality, a drinking straw one end of which has been dipped in soap. The other end is dipped in sugar and both ends of the straw are wiped so the secret preparation cannot be seen.

Place the matches near to the middle of the bowl. If you now put the soaped end of the straw to touch the water in the centre of the matches the soap will cause the matches to move outwards. When the other end of the straw is placed in the water the sugar pulls the matches back in to the centre.

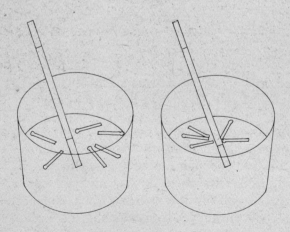

THE WATER DIVINER

In this trick you hold two matches between the first finger and thumb of one hand. As you move the matches towards a glass of water they move apart as if by magic. Even the word 'water' written on a piece of paper is sufficient to make this remarkable water diviner work.

What the spectators do not see is the fact that the matches are joined together at one end by a short piece of rubber tubing. The matches are held together with the fingers covering the rubber. By releasing the pressure of the fingers the tube begins to straighten out and the matches move apart.

rubber tubing

MATCH THROUGH METAL

For this trick you will need one match and a safety pin. Remove the head from the match. Get an adult to push the pin through the centre of the match. It is important that the match spins freely on the pin.

Flick one end of the match and it will appear that it passes right through the opposite bar of the pin.

What actually happens is that the match hits the bar

and then swings back so the opposite end comes up to the other side of the bar. This happens so fast that the eye is unable to follow the movement and the match appears to have passed through solid metal.

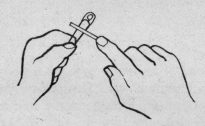

MULTIPLYING MATCHES

Empty a matchbox and secretly conceal three matches between the drawer and the outer case of the box. Place three matches in the box and you are ready to perform a nifty magic trick. Do not close the box or the trick will be ruined.

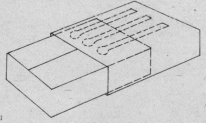

Show the three matches in the half open box. To convince your spectators there are only three matches tip them out on to a table. Now replace the three matches back in the drawer. At the same time make absolutely certain that everyone can see that there is nothing concealed in your hands.

Close the box.

Closing the box causes the three hidden matches to drop into the box. Make a magic pass over the box and ask someone to open it. When they do so they receive quite a surprise for it now contains twice as many matches as it did at the start.

A QUICK REVERSE

Cut the head off a match. Use a red pencil to colour one end of the match red. This colour should be only on the uppermost surface of the match. Turn the match over and colour the top surface of the opposite end of the match in similar fashion. Your finished match should look like the one shown in the illustration.

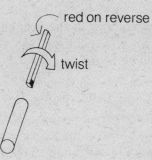
red on reverse

twist

In addition to the special match you will need a small paper tube. The length of the tube should be fractionally less than the length of the match. Its diameter should be just sufficient to take the match.

The trick is performed as follows. Show the match to the audience but make sure you show only the one side. Now show the tube and push the match, coloured end first, into it. As the match is pushed into the tube secretly give it a twist. When it emerges from the other end of the tube pull it out and it is seen that the colour has apparently jumped from one end of the match to the other.

Do it once more and then drop the match and the tube into your pocket.

There may be occasions when some people will want to have a go themselves. In readiness for such occasions it is worthwhile having a duplicate match in your pocket which has been coloured on one end only. Give this match to the enquiring spectator and he will never be able to work out how the trick was done.

END CHANGE

This trick takes quite a bit of practice to do properly but the effect is so good it will be worth persevering to get it right.

The effect is similar to the last trick but on this occasion the match is quite ordinary and your closed fist takes the place of the paper tube.

Allow your left hand to be seen empty and then close it into a loose fist. Hold your left hand with its back towards the audience.

With your right hand you pick up a match and push it, head downwards, into your left fist. You continue to push the match through the fist. Everything seems to be absolutely above board and yet when the match reappears its head is pointing up not down!

What actually happens is this. You push the match head downwards into your fist and into the crack between the first and second fingers. The illustration shows your view at this stage but you must be careful that no-one else sees this or you will give the trick away. Your right finger continues to push the match down and this causes it to revolve around your second finger so the non-striking end is now pointing downwards.

Remove the right forefinger for a split second and immediately reinsert it into the fist. This time the tip of the forefinger will come into contact with the head of the match. Push the match right through the fist and it emerges the opposite way round to the way it was put in.

When you can do this trick really well you may repeat it once or twice but do not overdo it or your spectators may begin to fathom out what has happened.

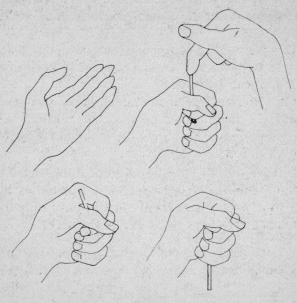

ONE IN THE POCKET

You show your audience three matches and break each one about ½ in (1.25 centimetres) from its head. Then you place two of the heads in your left hand and one in your right pocket. When you open your left hand you again have three heads in it. You then repeat the trick.

The secret of this trick is that you have a fourth match head hidden in your right hand right from the start.

Show the three match heads on the table. Pick up one with the right hand and drop it into your left. Now pick up the second head with your right hand and drop that into the left hand also. At the same time you secretly drop the concealed, fourth, head from the right hand into the left. There are now three heads in the left hand but the spectators think there are only two.

Now pick up the third head and pretend to place it in your right pocket. In fact you really keep it concealed in your right hand.

Ask someone how many match heads you have in your right hand. That person will naturally reply 'two', whereupon you open the hand and drop three match heads on the table.

You are now in a position to repeat the trick if you wish. On this second occasion really drop the last head into your pocket and then you will have only three match heads on view at the end of the trick.

THREE WAYS TO ACHIEVE THE IMPOSSIBLE

This little trick appears so simple and yet it is an absolute baffler. In fact it is so good I am giving you three different ways of achieving the same effect so the trick can be performed at any time and in any place. Because the trick is so good please do not give away any of the three methods — keep the trick a secret.

But what is the effect of this marvellous trick you may ask. This is what the spectators see: You show a match between the thumb and forefinger of each hand. When you bring the two matches together at right angles to each other, they seem to melt through one another and become interlocked. When the hands are drawn apart the matches again seem to pass through one another. No matter how close the spectators watch they can find no logical explanation as to how you can make solid pass through solid.

As mentioned above there are three methods that will bring about this unbelievable effect. For the first you will need two matches with red heads. Hold the matches as shown opposite but before doing so secretly wet the pad of one of your thumbs. When the match head is pressed against this wet area it will stick to the thumb.

Bring the two matches together and as they meet lift your forefinger away from the plain end of the stuck match, as shown in the illustration. This will open a gap just wide enough for you to pass the other match through. As soon as the other match has passed through the gap replace your forefinger and the matches are now interlocked. A reversal of these moves unlinks the matches.

Unfortunately, not all types of red match possess this adhesive quality. If you find this is the case with the matches you are using you will have to utilise one of the following methods, both of which use the same technique of providing a gap through which the other match can pass.

If one of the matches you use is broken off at the non-striking end there will be lots of tiny splinters in the end of the match. Press these splinters against the ball of your thumb and the match will cling to the thumb so the trick can be accomplished as in the first method.

The third method is not so convincing as the first two. It is, however, useful when you cannot utilise either of the previous methods. In this method you simply clip the end of one match between the first and second fingers of one hand. This enables you to release the thumb end of that match to provide a gap through which the other match can pass.

Whichever method you use, and it is worth learning all three, please practise the trick before showing it to anyone. With diligent practice this trick can give the appearance of pure magic and achieve for you a reputation as an expert magician.

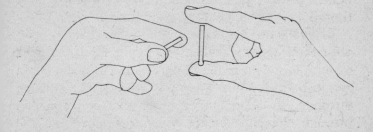

MATCHLESS VANISH

Ask someone to hold out their left hand. A match is then shown and it is touched against the spectator's hand three times. On the third time the spectator is to close his hand around the match — but as he does so the match disappears!

This trick requires some practice to do properly but the effect is so startling it will be well worth any effort you put into it. Each time you touch the spectator's hand with the match you make a large movement of it, bringing your hand down from quite a height each time. The third time you raise your hand you quickly slip the match into the hair at the side of your head. Without pausing bring your hand down to the spectator's once again. He tries to take the match but it has mysteriously disappeared.

If you are right handed it is best that you perform this trick with your left side towards the audience and vice versa.

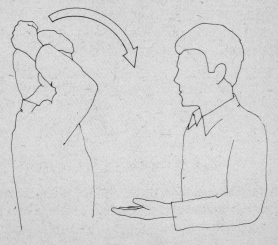

MAGNETIC MATCHES

You place one match on the table and then balance a second match across the first. Claiming that it is possible to cause matches to react like magnets you hold the third match between the ends of the other two. As you do so the top match swivels round as if moved by magnetism.

The trick is achieved by a simple but very subtle method. As everyone's attention is focused on the matches no-one will notice the fact that you are blowing on the matches. It is the power of your breath, not that of magnetism, that causes the top match to move!

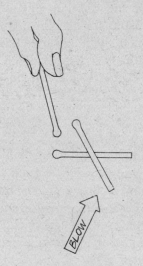

ANTI GRAVITY MATCHES

This trick requires a little advance preparation. Break a piece from the end of a match so it becomes possible to wedge that match in the drawer of a matchbox as shown. Replace the drawer in the sleeve and you are ready to defy the law of gravity.

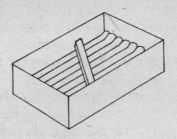

Show the box of matches to your audience. Push the drawer out about halfway so everyone can see the matches inside. In doing this make sure you do not expose the wedged match.

Now turn the box over so the drawer is upside down and slowly pull the drawer from the sleeve. Because of the secret wedged match the matches do not fall out. If your wedged match is not a very good fit hold the drawer on either side and press inwards to prevent the wedged match from slipping.

At this point some spectators will begin to think that you are using some form of trick matchbox and that the matches are no longer in the drawer. To reassure them that this is not the case you shake the drawer and everyone will hear the matches rattle.

Now pretend to remove your magical influence and give the drawer a sharp downward shake. This will dislodge the wedged match and all the matches will fall from the drawer. As the short match you used as a wedge is now lost among the other matches the audience is left with no clue as to how the trick was accomplished.

A RATTLING GOOD TRICK

You place three matchboxes on a table; two are empty and the third appears to contain matches. When you mix the boxes up on the table your spectators will never be able to find the full box no matter how hard they watch your actions. You can repeat this trick several times but your audience will never pick the right box. The spectators never succeed due to the simple fact that all three matchboxes are empty. What people do not notice is that you shake the empty boxes with your right hand and the apparently full box with your left hand. You do this because attached to your left wrist by an elastic band is a fourth box containing some matches. The presence of this secret box is concealed by your sleeve. You can make any of the three boxes on the table appear to contain matches simply by picking it up and shaking it with the left hand. No-one will realise that the sound is not coming from that box.

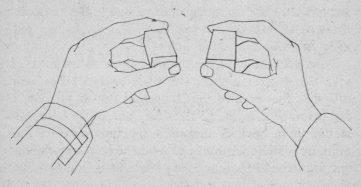

COME TOGETHER

Put one match in each hand and then hold the hands apart. Now announce to the gathered spectators that you can get both matches into one hand without bringing the hands together.

If you have previously performed some of the other tricks in this chapter everyone will think you are going to do this by magic — but you do not, you cheat.

All you do is drop the match from the left hand on to the table. Now, keeping your hands spread wide apart, you turn around until your right hand is above the table. Pick up the match with your right hand. You now have both matches in your right hand and yet you did not bring your hands together.

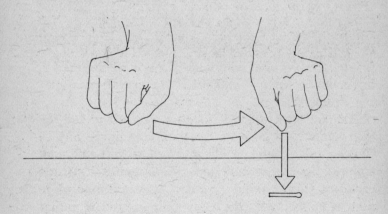

ESTIMATION

While your back is turned a spectator counts the number of matches in a box. When he has done this he is asked to add together the two digits of the number arrived at and to remove that number of matches from the pile. The remaining matches are replaced in the box and the box is closed.

You now turn back around, pick up the box, and shake it. Then, much to the surprise of the spectators, you announce the exact number of matches inside the box.

Yes, this trick can be performed with a borrowed box of matches. In fact, it is more effective if you have not seen or handled the box before your performance.

The secret of this trick depends upon two subtle principles. The first is that if the digits of a number are totalled and then taken away from the number the result is always a multiple of nine. Thus if the original figure is 47 the two digits (4 and 7) total 11, which then subtracted from 47 give 36, a multiple of nine. As a result, no matter how many matches were in the box at the start there will only be five possible answers at the finish (the average contents of a box of matches is normally between 40 and 50) These answers are 9, 18, 27, 36 and 45.

All you have to do is to train yourself to tell the difference in sound when a box containing any of these totals is shaken. That is not so difficult as it sounds. Put nine matches in a box and rattle it. Listen carefully to the sound it makes. Now add nine more matches and rattle the box – the sound is rather different. With a bit of practice you will find that you will know immediately whether the box contains 9, 18, 27, 36 or 45 matches.

Once you can differentiate between these five distinct sounds you can begin to show people this amazing trick.

CHICKEN RAID

This trick is very easy to do — in fact it works itself — but because it is woven into a little story it is both entertaining and baffling.

Lay seven matches on the table to represent seven chickens. Beneath these place two more matches to represent tramps.

You pick up the two tramps, one in each hand, and then relate this story: 'One day two tramps approached a farm where they saw some chickens. Realising that the chickens would make a fine meal they decided to share them and they began stuffing the poor unfortunate birds into their pockets' (as you say this you pick up one of the chickens in your right hand, the next in your left, and so on alternately until all the chickens have been picked up.)

'At this point they saw the farmer approaching so they decided to put the chickens back' (Place down a match alternately from each hand, starting with the *left* hand, until there are seven matches on the table once again. Keep your hands closed for at this point the spectators will assume you have one match, or tramp, in each hand. In fact you have two matches in your right hand and none in your left)

'When the farmer went away they shared out the chickens once again'. (Again pick up the chickens, one at a time, alternately, starting with the right hand).

'They ran from the farm as fast as they could but a little way down the road they had a fight and this tramp (place down a match from the left hand) got the worst of the argument and ended up with only two

78

chickens (place down two matches from the left hand and show the hand empty.) This tramp (place down a match from the right hand) won the argument and ended up with five chickens (count out five matches from the right hand).

Although you have done nothing very clever you will often be credited with having performed an amazing feat of sleight of hand when you demonstrate this trick.

MATCH PLAY

MATCHING EYES

Make two small discs of paper and push a match through the centre of each disc until just the head is visible. Close your right hand into a loose fist. Push the matches in between the third and fourth fingers and then drape a handkerchief over your hand. You have now produced a reasonable representation of a face and you can make its mouth open and close simply by moving your thumb.

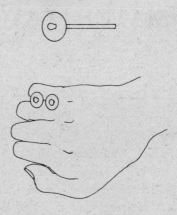

If you can speak without moving your lips you will be able to give the impression that the face you have created can talk.

BOXES

There is a very popular game called boxes, or dots and squares, which is played with pencil and paper. It is also possible to play the game with matches. Any number of players can take part but each one will need about thirty matches.

The players take it in turns to lay matches down on the table. Every match laid must touch at least one of the matches already on the table and must be at an angle of 90° or 180° to it. The object of the game is to form squares and also to prevent the other players from doing so.

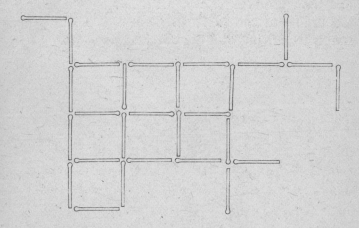

When a player completes a square he is allowed to place down an additional match. Each square formed scores one point and the player who has the highest number of points when all the matches have been played is, of course, the winner.

GUESS THE TOTAL

This is a game for two or more players. Each player is given three matches. Each player hides from none to three matches in his right hand and extends that hand towards the centre of the group.

The players now take it in turns to guess the total number of matches being held. When everyone has had a guess the hands are opened and the matches are counted. The person whose guess was closest to the actual total wins a point.

After a predetermined number of rounds the player with the most points is the winner.

All the guesses must be different, no two players may guess the same number.

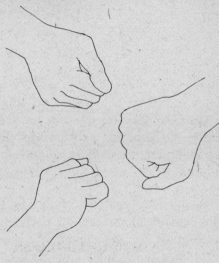

DIGITAL DEXTERITY

Place five matches on the table. Pick up the first match between your thumbs as shown. Pick up the second match between your first fingers taking care not to drop the first match as you do so. The third match is picked up between the second fingers, the fourth match between the third fingers, and the fifth between the little fingers.

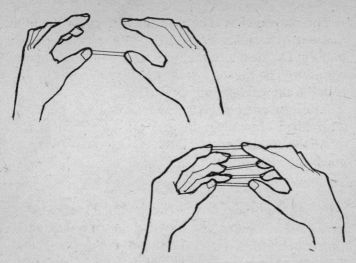

When you have managed to do this successfully replace the matches, one at a time, on the table.

Organise a competition with your friends and see who can complete the whole sequence in the shortest possible time.

INDIAN HEAD-DRESS

Collect some large leaves and as many spent matches as you can find. With these simple properties you are all set to become a Red Indian chief.

Take two of the leaves and place one on top of the other so they overlap slightly. Now push a match through both the leaves near the top. Straighten the match and then push it back through both the leaves near the bottom. The two leaves are now threaded together by the match.

85

matches pin leaves together

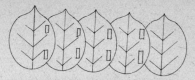

for a belt pin leaves this way

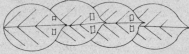

If you continue this process with several other leaves you will eventually have a string of leaves that is long enough to go round your head. Pin the last leaf to the first and you have an effective Red Indian head-dress.

A belt can be made in the same way but you will find this easier if you pin the leaves together lengthways as shown in the second illustration.

COTTON REEL CANNON

Get an old wooden cotton reel, a strong elastic band, and a couple of drawing pins.

Use the drawing pins to secure the elastic band around one end of the cotton reel. The elastic band should be stretched reasonably taut.

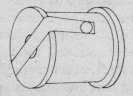

band secured by drawing pins

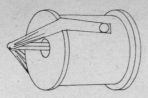

match pulled back to fire

Push a matchstick into the hole in the other end of the cotton reel and push the elastic band until you can grasp it with your other hand. Now use that hand to pull both the elastic and the match back, rather like using a bow and arrow. When you release your hold the match will shoot forward like a cannon ball from a cannon.

This cannon should be used only to shoot at toys or targets made from cardboard. Never point it at a person or an animal. It could be dangerous.

GOING FOR A WALK

Get an adult to make a short split in the ends of two matches. Now push the split ends together as shown.

Place the joined matches over the blade of a dinner knife held level with a table top. Allow the ends of the matches to just touch the table top.

87

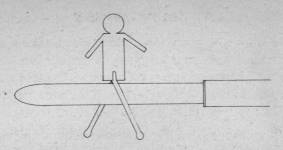

No matter how still you hold the knife the matches will begin to 'walk' along it. This is because you are making slight involuntary muscle movements which, magnified by the knife, cause the matches to move.

By fixing a flat card body into the top of the matches you can make a little man to walk along the blade.

MATCH BOAT

Get an adult to split the end of a match as shown in the illustration. Place the match in a bowl of water and drop a small amount of washing up liquid into the split end of the match.

The match will now move forward of its own accord, propelled by the washing up liquid.

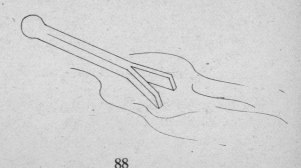

TUMBLING TOWER

Any number of people can play this excellent game from which you can derive a great deal of fun. Apart from the players all you need is a box of matches and a wine glass. Place all the matches in the wine glass with their heads uppermost and you are ready to start.

The first player removes a match from the glass and rests it horizontally upon the remaining matches. Each player now takes turns to do the same. At first this procedure is quite simple but as the number of vertical matches goes down and the horizontal pile gets higher the whole structure gets rather precarious. Every match added to the pile weakens its foundations.

Whenever a match is dislodged and falls on the table the offending player loses a point.

Eventually the whole pile will collapse and the player who causes this downfall loses five points.

The player with the least penalty points after the collapse of the pagoda, as the pile is called, is the winner.

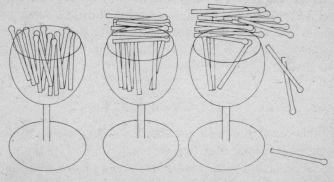

IN THE SAUCER

A saucer is placed on the floor a short distance away.

The players now take it in turns to throw matches at the saucer. After each player's turn the matches that have landed on the saucer are counted.

When everyone has had a go it is the person with the highest score who is the winner.

This game is not always as easy as it sounds. You will find that it is relatively easy to hit the saucer. But in a large number of cases the matches do not stay there but simply bounce off.

THE LAST OF ELEVEN

Place eleven matches on a table. Two players now take it in turns to remove either one, two or three matches. The person who has to take the last match is the loser.

It is possible for you to win this game every time. All you have to do is to make sure that you pick up the sixth match.

This will leave five matches on the table. If your opponent now picks up one match you take three, if he takes two you take two, and if he takes three you take one, so that whatever happens there is always one match remaining for your opponent – and he loses the game!

THE LAST OF FIFTEEN

This is exactly the same as the last game except for the fact that fifteen matches are used.

Once again it is possible for you to win every time.

In this instance the winning secret is to make sure that on one of your goes you leave exactly nine matches on the table. On your next go you must ensure that no less than five matches remain on the table and you can then force your opponent to take the last match. Once again he is the loser.

THE LAST OF TWENTY FIVE

This game is the same as the last two but on this occasion the players can remove from one to four matches at a time. A total of twenty five matches is used and the person who has to take the last match is the loser.

Again it is possible for you to win every time. To do this you must take your matches in such a way that after you go there are 21, 16, 11 or at least six matches on the table.

THE LAST OF THIRTY

Here is yet another game based on a similar theme to the last three. This one uses thirty matches and the two players take it in turns to remove from one to six matches. On this occasion, however, it is the person who takes the last match who is the winner.

As with the previous games there is a simple way to ensure that you can win. It is obvious that if on the last go your opponent has to draw from seven matches no matter how many are taken you can pick up the last match. By the same token if you can leave 28, 21, or 14 matches after you have taken your turn you can win every time.

MATCH BOX

I have always envied people who have the patience and ability to make intricate models from matches. Although I can demonstrate infinite patience in several chosen spheres model making is not one of them. But, on the other hand, I have always believed that I could make some interesting things with matchsticks if I set my mind to it.

Many years ago I discovered a simple but effective technique that enables even the ham-fisted like me to make match models that look as if they require a great deal of skill to make. In actual fact they are quite easy to do. The technique I discovered is simply to make a paper model of the thing you wish to make and then to glue matches to it.

Here is a simple box which I hope will give you some idea of how easy it all is. Once you have made this box you can progress to more elaborate items.

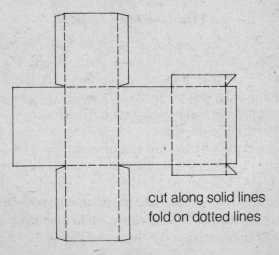

cut along solid lines
fold on dotted lines

From thin card cut out the shape shown in the illustration. No measurements have been given as these will be determined by the size of the box you wish to make. For your first effort, however, I suggest that the depth of your box be slightly more than the length of the matchsticks (with their heads cut off). The length should be exactly the length of the matchsticks and the width can be whatever you wish.

Fold the card into the shape of a box. Now put the glue on one side of the box and stick matches to it. Do the same with all the other sides. For the sides of the lid it is best to cut the matches to the correct length before gluing them into position. In the majority of cases this is the best method to adopt whenever you are doing anything that is slightly awkward.

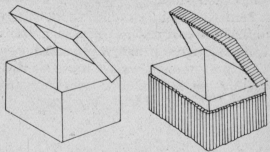

If you wish you could also glue matches to the inside of the box. What I normally do is to cover the inside with felt.

LOG HUT

Using the same basic technique as for the match box just described it is possible to build a wide variety of different buildings. To make a simple log hut, for example, all you need is a card shape like that shown in the illustration. Matches are glued to it as for the box. The only thing you have to remember is to leave spaces for the windows.

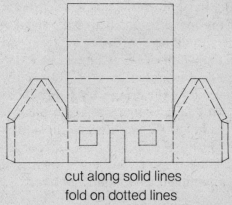

cut along solid lines
fold on dotted lines

If you wish you could make a hut like this in which the door can be opened. If you wish to do this you will find that the matches for the door have to be cut slightly shorter than the width of the door to allow it to open.

Using this basic design it is possible to build quite a wide variety of houses and other buildings.

The house can easily be painted or coated with clear varnish to give it a professional finish.

THE ANSWERS

SQUARES AND TRIANGLES

page 8 **FIVE FROM FOUR**

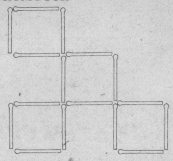

page 8 **REMOVE FOUR TO MAKE FOUR**

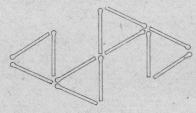

page 9 **FOUR FROM FIVE**

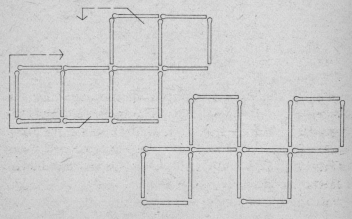

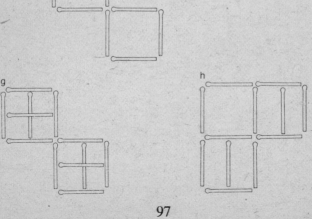

a

b

c

d

e

f

g

h

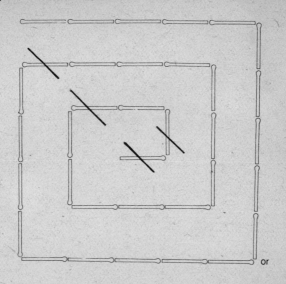

or

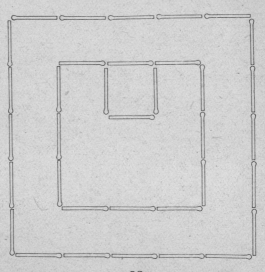

98

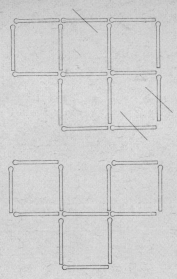

When the appropriate matches are removed the following arrangements are obtained in answer to each problem.

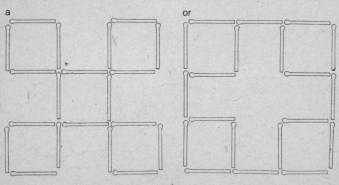

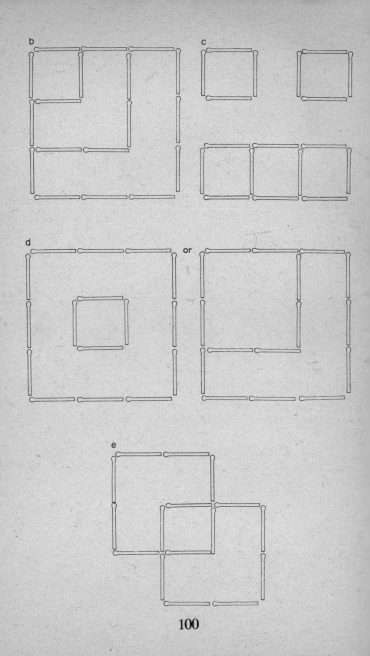

b

c

d

or

e

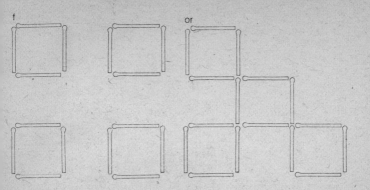

page 12   **JUST TWENTY FOUR**

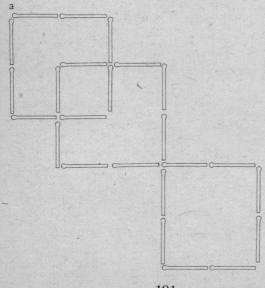

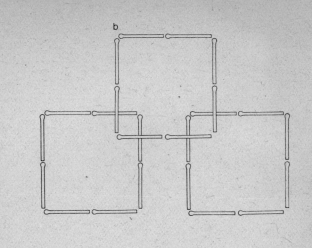

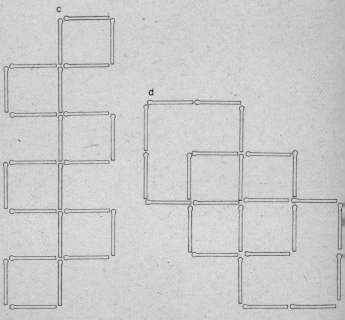

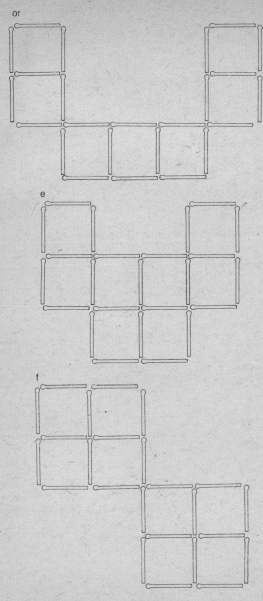

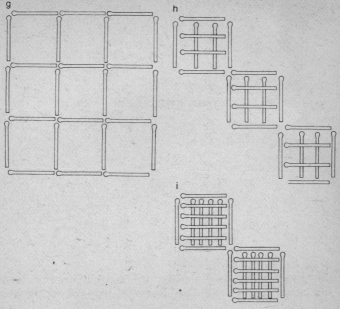

page 12　ELIMINATE THE SQUARES

a Thirty squares

b Nine matches is the lowest number you must remove as shown below.

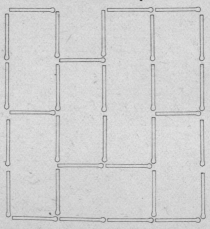

page 13 **THREE TO TWO**

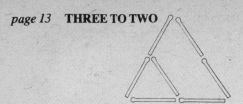

page 14 **TRIANGLES IN A HEXAGON**

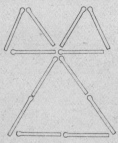

page 14 **FIVE FROM THREE**

Simply dismantle one of the outer triangles and reform it beneath the other two. You now have four small triangles and the whole shape forms the fifth triangle.

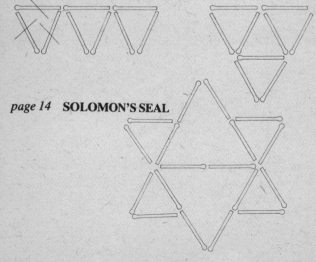

page 14 **SOLOMON'S SEAL**

A TRICKY PROBLEM

The trick is to break four of the matches in half so that the three squares can now be formed as shown below.

REMOVE THREE TO MAKE THREE

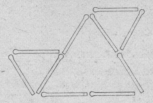

SQUARE TRICK

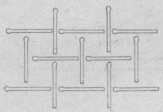

AXE TRIANGLES

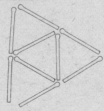

DIAMOND DAZZLER

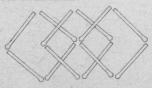

page 17 **TURN THE L**

Move the matches from the positions indicated by the dotted lines
and place them as shown.

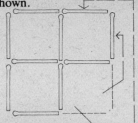

page 17 **HOW TO MAKE DIAMONDS**

Move the matches as indicated by the dotted lines and replace
them as shown. This forms four diamonds and the large, outer
diamond makes the fifth.

page 18 **MAKE NINE**

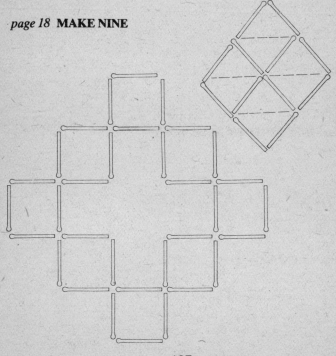

page 18 **TRICKY TRIANGLE**

Place the match on the corner of a table, or something similar, so the table forms two sides of the triangle and the match completes the third side.

page 19 **TRICKY SQUARE**

Place the two matches on the corner of a table. The matches form two sides of the square and the edges of the table form the other two sides.

page 19 **SQUARES AND TRIANGLES**

Arrange the eight matches as shown.

108

ROMAN ARITHMETIC

page 23 **4−2 =5**
Take one of the matches forming the figure 2 and use it to change
the minus sign into a plus sign. The equation now reads 4 +1 =5
which is correct.

page 23 **3=1**

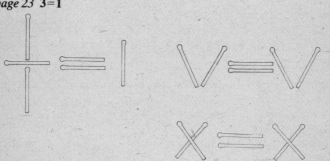

page 23 **3−2=4**
Take the vertical match from the 4 and place it on the minus sign to
make it a plus. You now have 3 + 2 = 5.

page 24 **6 − 4 =9**

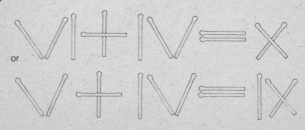

page 24 **1 − 3 = 2**

page 24 **7 − 2 = 2**

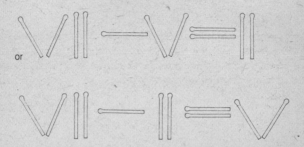

page 25 **11 + 1 = 10**
Just move around the table and view the equation from the other side!

page 25 **7 − 1 = 1**
Simply remove the two matches forming the V in the number 7. The equation now reads 2 − 1 = 1 which is correct.

page 25 **10 + 10 = 10**

110

page 26 **6 + 2 = 5**

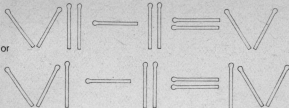

or

page 26 **3 − 5 = 2**

Move one of the matches from the equals sign on the right to make it into a minus sign. Replace the match above the original minus sign on the left to change it into an equals sign. The equation now reads 3 = 5 − 2 which is correct.

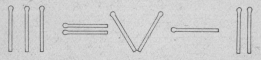

page 26 **HALF A DOZEN**

First arrange eight matches to form the Roman numeral XII (12), as shown on page 26. If you now remove the four matches that form the lower half of the figure, you are left with VII, the Roman numeral for seven. You have thus proved that half of twelve is seven!

PERPLEXING PROBLEMS

page 28 **THE BUILDING PLOT**

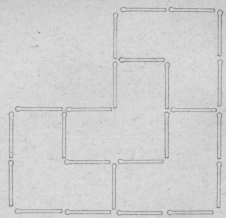

page 28 **TREASURE ISLAND**

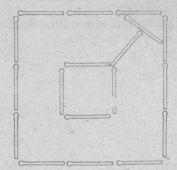

page 29 **ANOTHER BRIDGE**

Use the four matches to make the bridge as shown below.

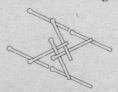

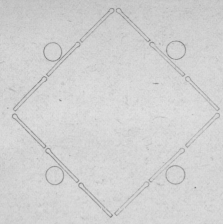

page 31 **REMOVE THE STRAW**

The sequence below shows how to remove the straw in two moves. Although it is now upside down the glass remains intact as stipulated.

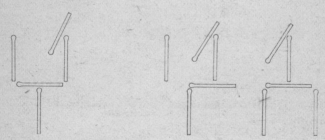

page 31 **CROSS SOLITAIRE**

There are two possible sequences that can be followed to obtain the four crosses as stipulated:

	or
Place match 5 on 2	Place match 4 on 7
Place match 3 on 7	Place match 6 on 2
Place match 1 on 4	Place match 1 on 3
Place match 8 on 6	Place match 8 on 5

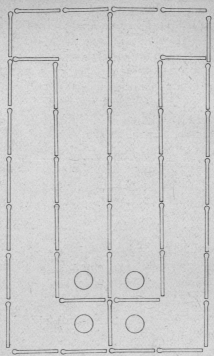

page 33 **FOUR PILES**

Imagine the matches numbered from one to twelve and make the following moves:

Move 7 to 3
Move 5 to 10
Move 9 to 3
Move 12 to 8
Move 4 to 10
Move 11 to 8
Move 2 to 6
Move 1 to 6

page 33 **FOUR PAIRS**

Move 4 over 5 and 6 and place it next to 7
Move 6 over 5 and 3 and place it next to 2
Move 1 over 2 and its partner and place it next to 3
Move 5 over 7 and its partner and place it next to 8
The matches now form four pairs as shown. The number beneath
each match represents its position in the original line up.

page 34 **EVEN REMOVAL**

Remove the matches from the position shown.

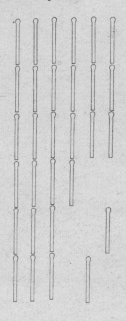

Rearrange the matches as shown. The extra match is added to the centre number to form the letter O.

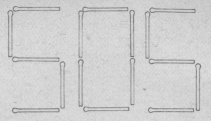

OIL TO INK

page 36 **MATCHEMATICS**

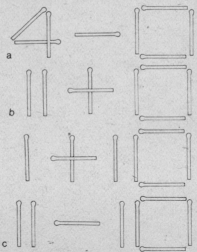

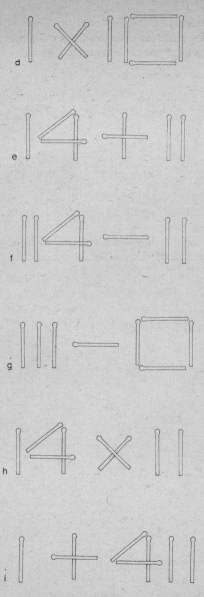

117

page 36 **ARITHMATCHIC**

Take the first match and place it on the minus sign to change it into a plus sign and you have 4 + 1 which equals five.

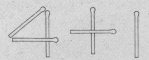

page 37 **5 + 4 = 6**

a Move the match from the top left of the six to change it into the number nine.

b Move the top left match of the five to the right and the bottom left of the five to the left and the five changes into a two.

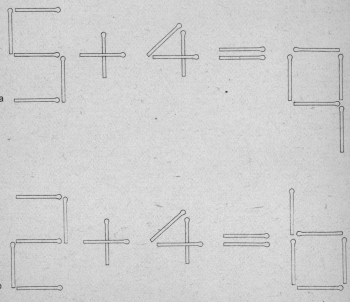

page 37 **2 + 9 = 8**
Move the match forming the tail of the nine to the top left of that
figure to change it into the number six.

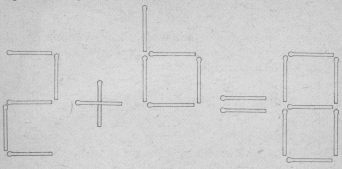

page 38 **3 + 2 = 6**
Move the match on the left edge of the two to the right to make it
into a three.

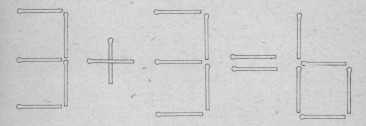

page 39 **6 + 3 = 3**

a Take the match from the base of the second three and place it at the top left edge to make it into the number nine.

b Remove one of the matches from the plus sign to make it into a minus sign.

c Move the two matches on the left edge of the six to make it into a three. Then move the top two matches of the second three to make it into the number six.

page 39 **2 + 1 = 8**

The two matches are removed from the left side of the eight to make it into the number 3.

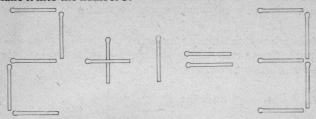

page 39 **DO NOT TOUCH**

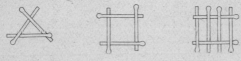

page 39 **PENS FOR PIGS**

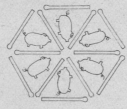

page 40 **UPS AND DOWNS**

Move 2nd and 3rd matches to positions 7 and 8
Move 3rd and 4th matches to positions 2 and 3
Move 6th and 7th matches to positions 5 and 6
Move 1st and 2nd matches to positions 6 and 7

page 40 **COIN MATCH**

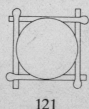

page 41 **GROUPS OF THREE**

Place match 5 on 1
Place match 6 on 1
Place match 9 on 3
Place match 10 on 3
Place match 8 on 14

now continue with either of the following sequences

4 on 13	7 on 14
11 on 14	4 on 2
15 on 13	11 on 2
7 on 2	13 on 15
12 on 2	12 on 15

page 41 **A FARMER'S PROBLEM**

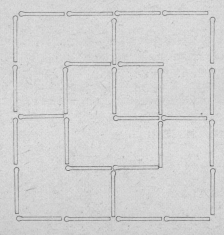

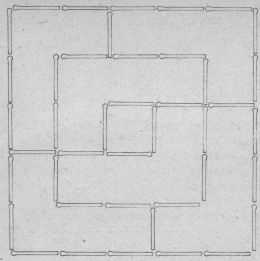

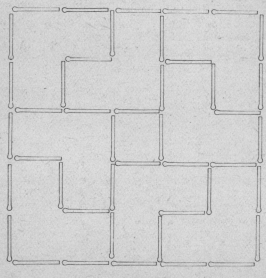

page 44 STAR TURN

All you have to do is allow a few drops of water to fall on the centre of the cross. The matches will then move of their own accord and form the star. This works best on a smooth surface.

page 44 ROBBING THE BANK

This has to be done on a table covered with a tablecloth. With your fingernails scratch the cloth near one of the uppermost matches forming the bank and the coin will crawl out under it.

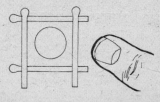

page 44 ICE PICK

All you have to do is to rest the match on the ice cube and then sprinkle salt over it. This will cause the match and the cube to freeze together so when you lift the match the cube comes too!

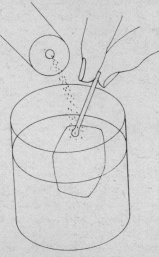

page 45 **A TRICKY ONE**

The trick is that the four matches are added to the five removed (not to the six remaining) to form a pile of nine matches.

page 45 **TRIANGLE TEASER**

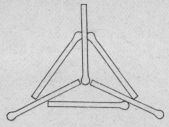

page 45 **ABSOLUTELY NOTHING**

page 46 **IMPOSSIBLE SQUARE**

A crafty one, this! Simply move the right horizontal match a fraction to the right. A square is thus formed in the centre of the cross.

page 46 **IMPOSSIBLE LIFT**

Lay one match down on the table. Now place seven matches so that one end of each match rests on the first match as shown. The remaining match is placed across the matches on the table as shown. If the first match is now lifted the seven matches will drop into a cross formation held in place by the top match.

As the positioning of the matches is very important you should try this out in private before showing it to anyone else.

The longer the matches used the easier is this trick to do.

page 47 **NUMBER PROBLEMS**

page 48 **LIFT THEM**

Very carefully push the V into an upright position using the fourth match. The third match will then slip down so its end falls through the angle of the V. When this happens the fourth match can be raised and the three matches will be lifted.

To do this requires a steady hand and some patience. It is worth practising the stunt in private before showing it to anyone else.

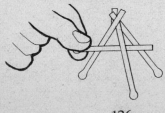

page 48 **CRAFTY LIFT**

Leave the pile of matches in the box and ram the additional match in between the drawer and the sleeve of the box. By lifting the single match you lift the full box as well.

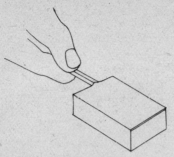

Page 48 **OPEN UP**

All you have to do is to allow one or two drops of water to fall on the broken centre of the match. In a short while the two ends of the match will open magically to allow the coin to drop into the bottle.

Arrange the matches as shown below:

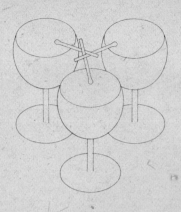